Joy
Terry Kelley
Mark Harris

to all teachers who create a safe place
for children to learn and grow

$12.95

Harrison, Marvel • Kellogg, Terry • Michaels, Greg

ISBN 1-880257-00-9

Printed in the United States of America

Other books offered by BRAT Publishing:

Finding Balance *12 Priorities For Interdependence and Joyful Living:*
Terry Kellogg & Marvel Harrison

Broken Toys Broken Dreams *Understanding and Healing Boundaries, Codependence,
Compulsion & Family Relationships:* Terry Kellogg

AttrACTIVE WOMEN *A Physical Fitness Approach To Emotional & Spiritual Well-Being:*
Marvel Harrison & Catharine Stewart-Roache

Butterfly Kisses *Little Intimacies For Sharing!* Harrison & Kellogg & Michaels

Hummingbird Words *Self Affirmations & Notes To Nurture By:* Harrison & Kellogg & Michaels

Roots & Wings *Words For Growing A Family:* Harrison & Kellogg & Michaels

BRAT Publishing, Suite 225, 6 University Drive, Amherst, MA 01002
1-800-359-BRAT (2728)

hummingbird words
affirmations for your spirit to soar
and notes to nurture by

marvel harrison   terry kellogg

illustrations by greg michaels

BRAT PUBLISHING

*h*ave you ever been with someone who fully accepted you with their words and presence? they know the joy and share the treasure of hummingbird words. as a field of blossoms gives energy to a hummingbird flight, these words nourish our soul and set our spirit to soar.

*h*ummingbird words are small prayers to read, say and hear so we can believe, feel and share. they are gifts we give to ourselves and others to tickle, entertain, heal and nurture.

*e*ach affirmation adds one more verse to the expanding hymn of the universe.

i am spirited

i choose my own path

i like what i do, not do what i like

i find elegance in simplicity

i am not changing - i am becoming

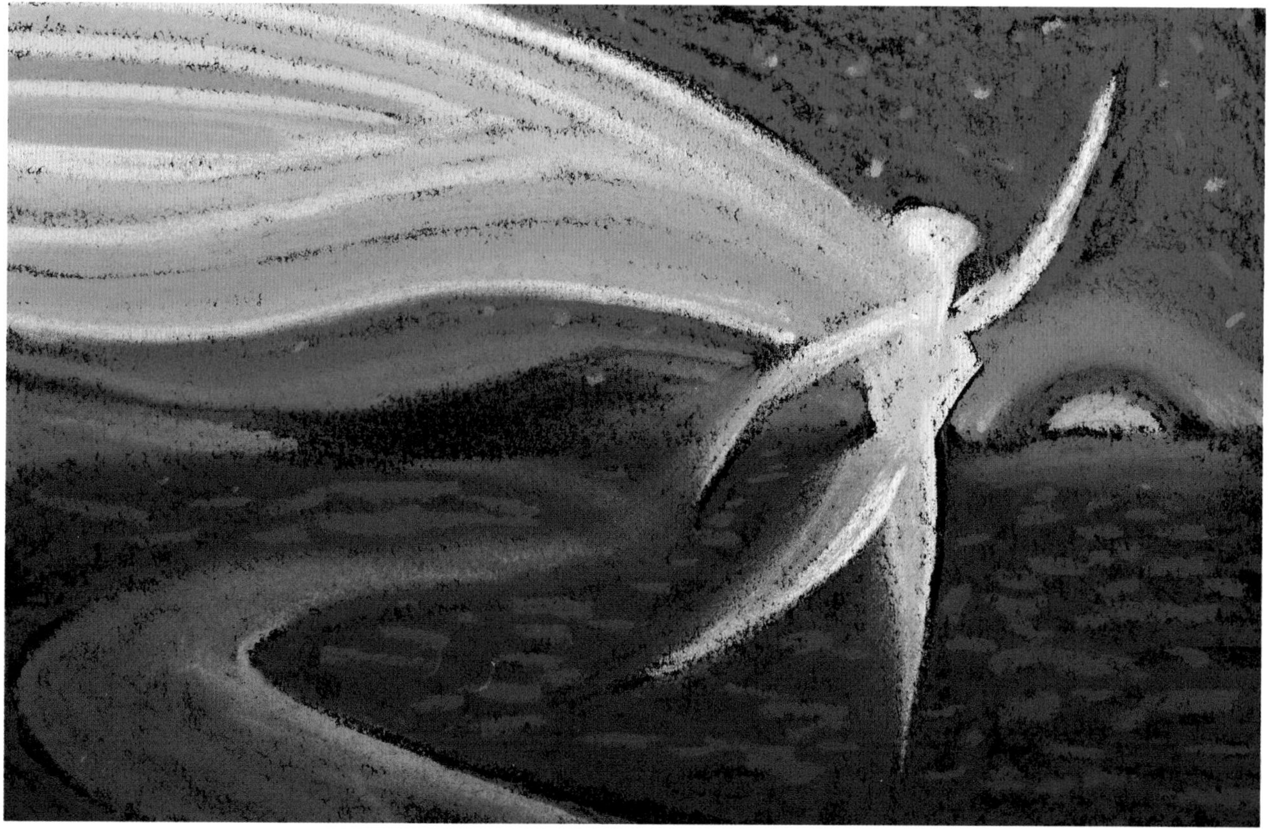

You please me
you are a blessing in my life
your caring makes a difference
it is a joy to know you

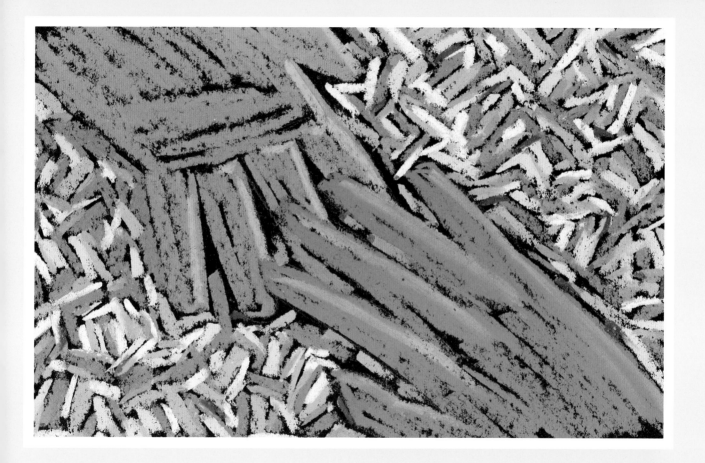

i am a precious and unique being

my humor heals me

i am gentle

my life is a puddle wading journey

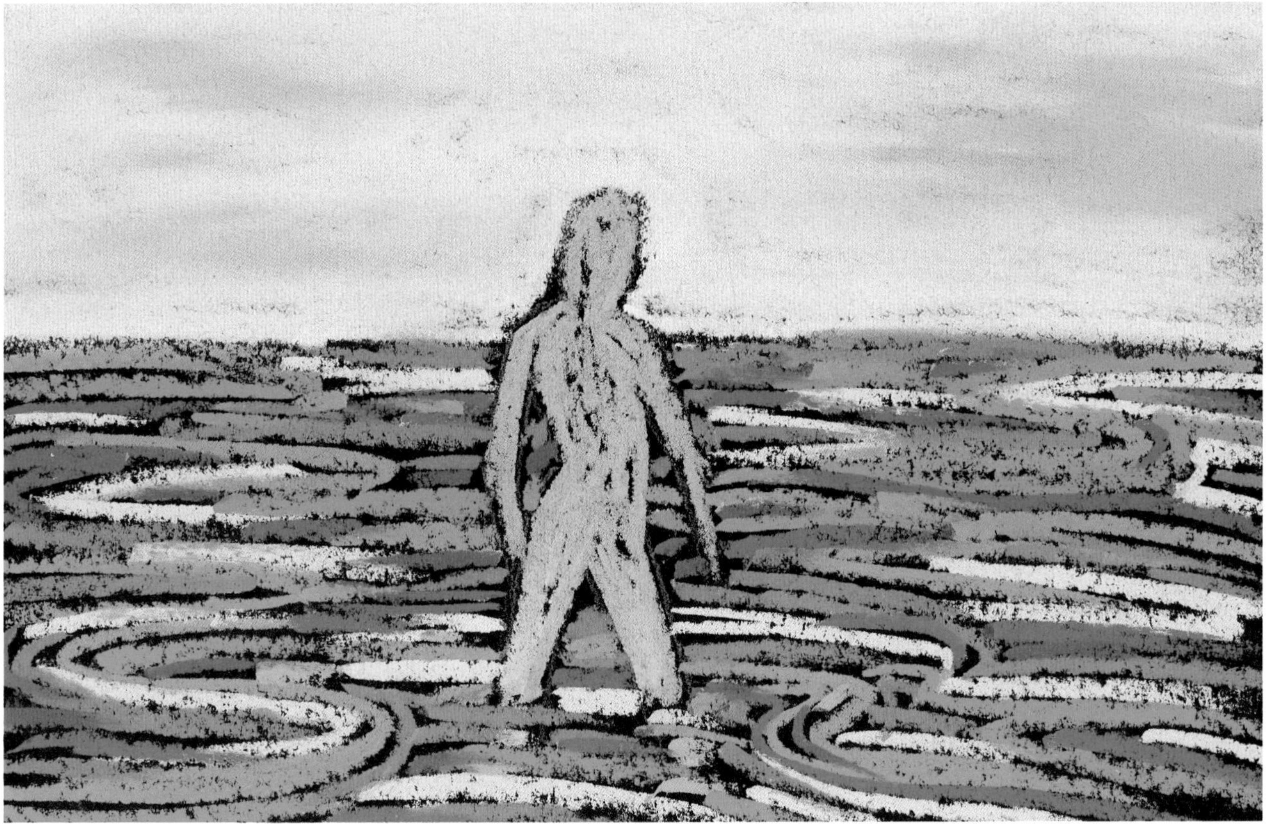

i value your stories

you notice the little things

you live your values

your tenderness is a treasure

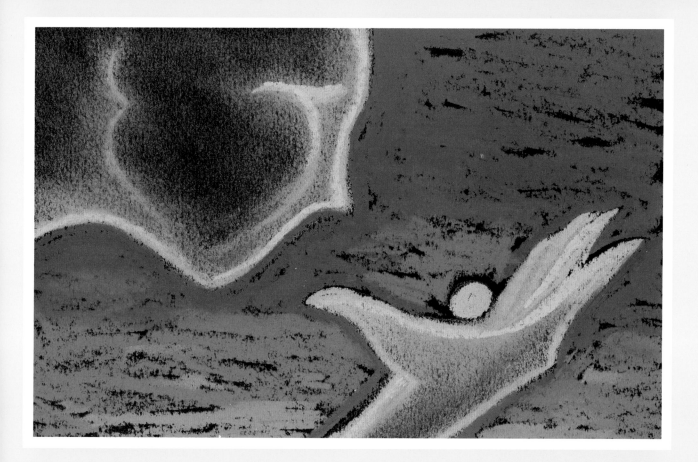

*m*y body is a temple

caring for my body gives me a place to worship

listening to my body brings me wisdom

challenging my body fulfills my potential

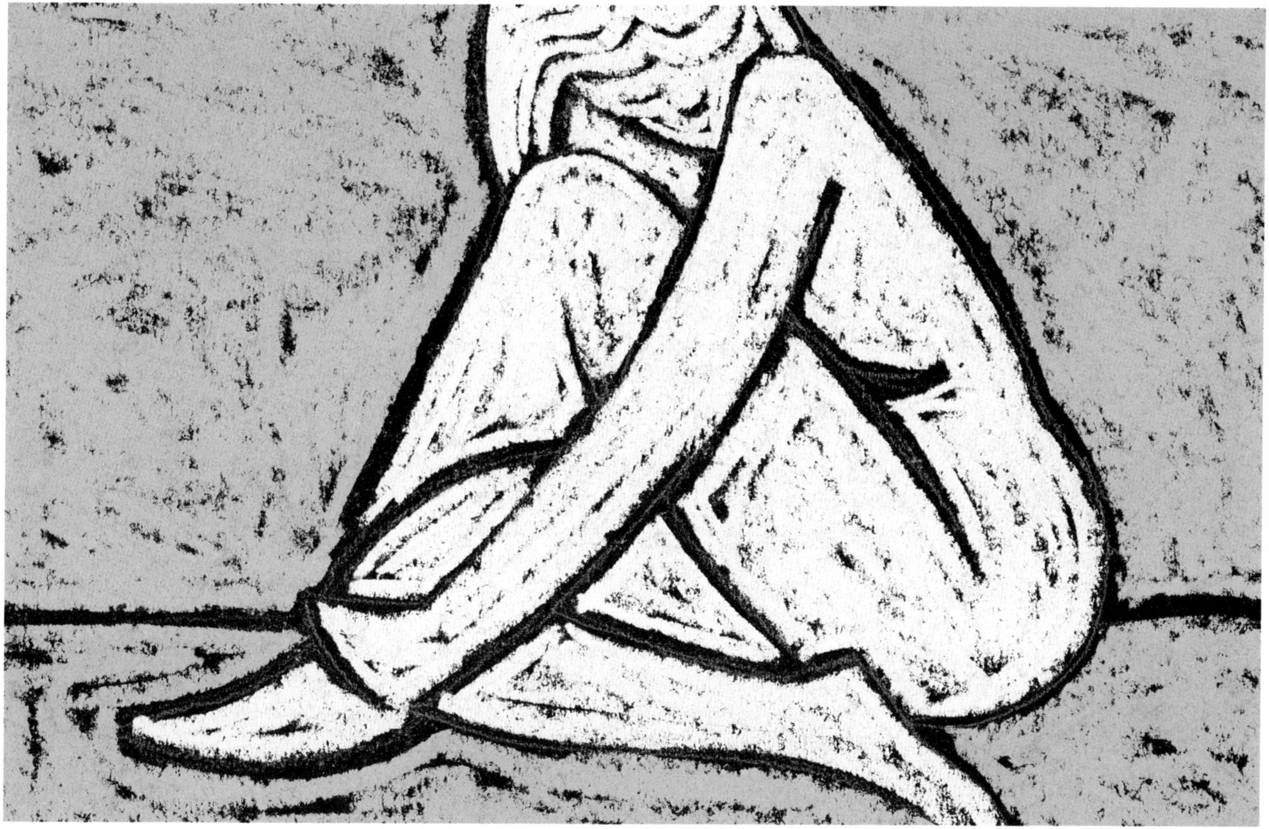

i feel warm in your presence

i believe you are doing your best

your touch tingles

you give from who you are

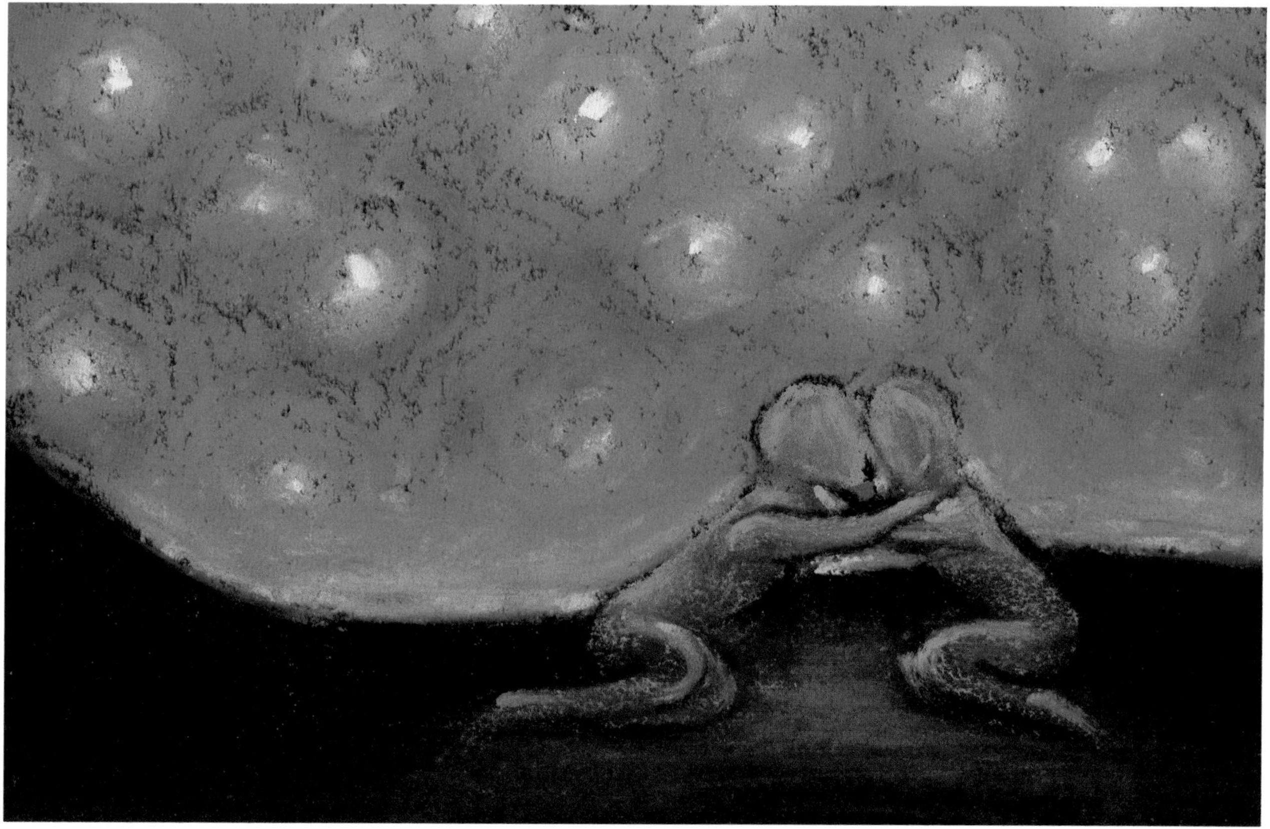

Your playful spirit enlivens

your voice is wind song

your eyes sparkle

you are a keeper

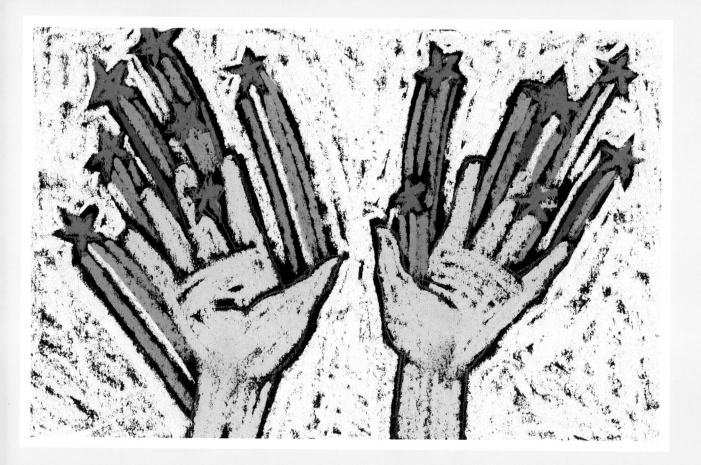

i make good decisions

i cherish my inner brat

my creativity brings me joy

i forgive me

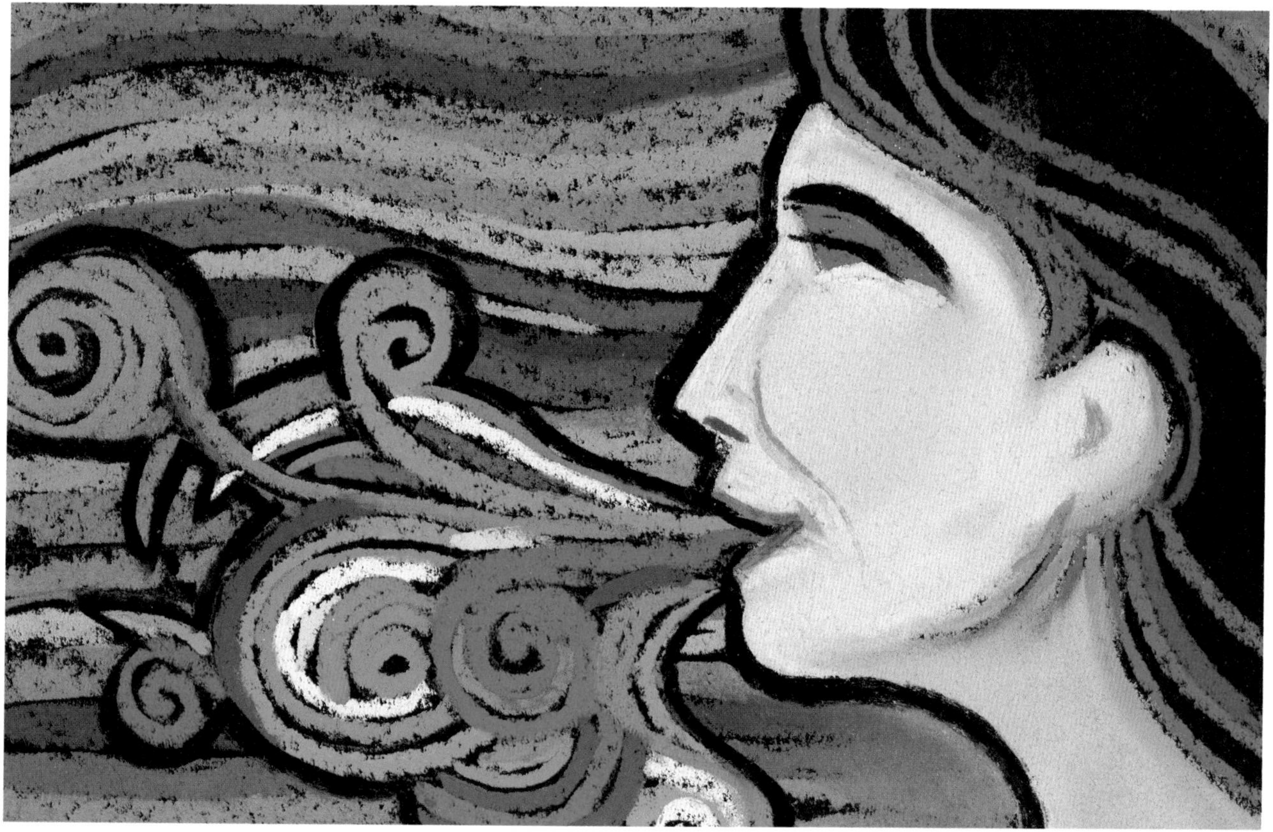

You do magic

your song touches children of all ages

your children reflect your nurturing

your kids did a great job of planned parenthood

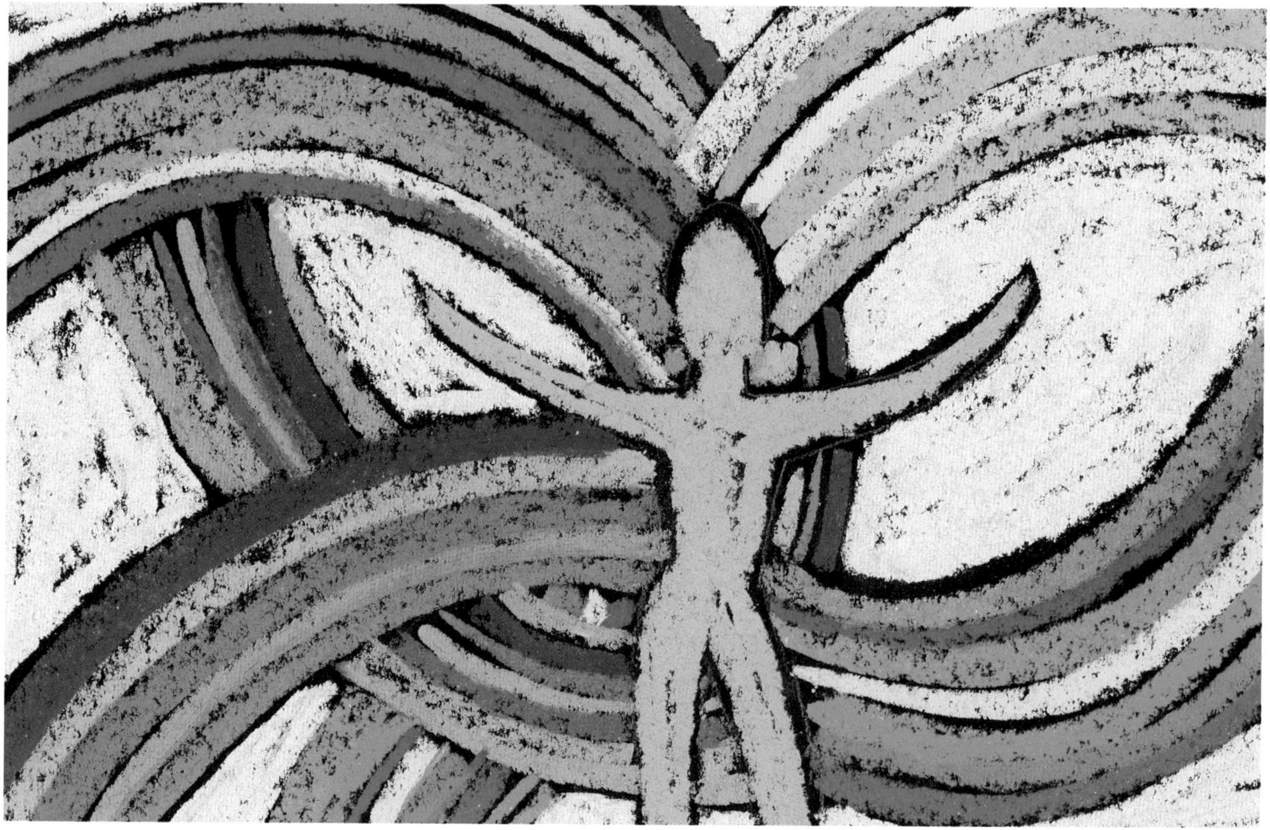

i am affable

i am laughable

i am capable

i am educable

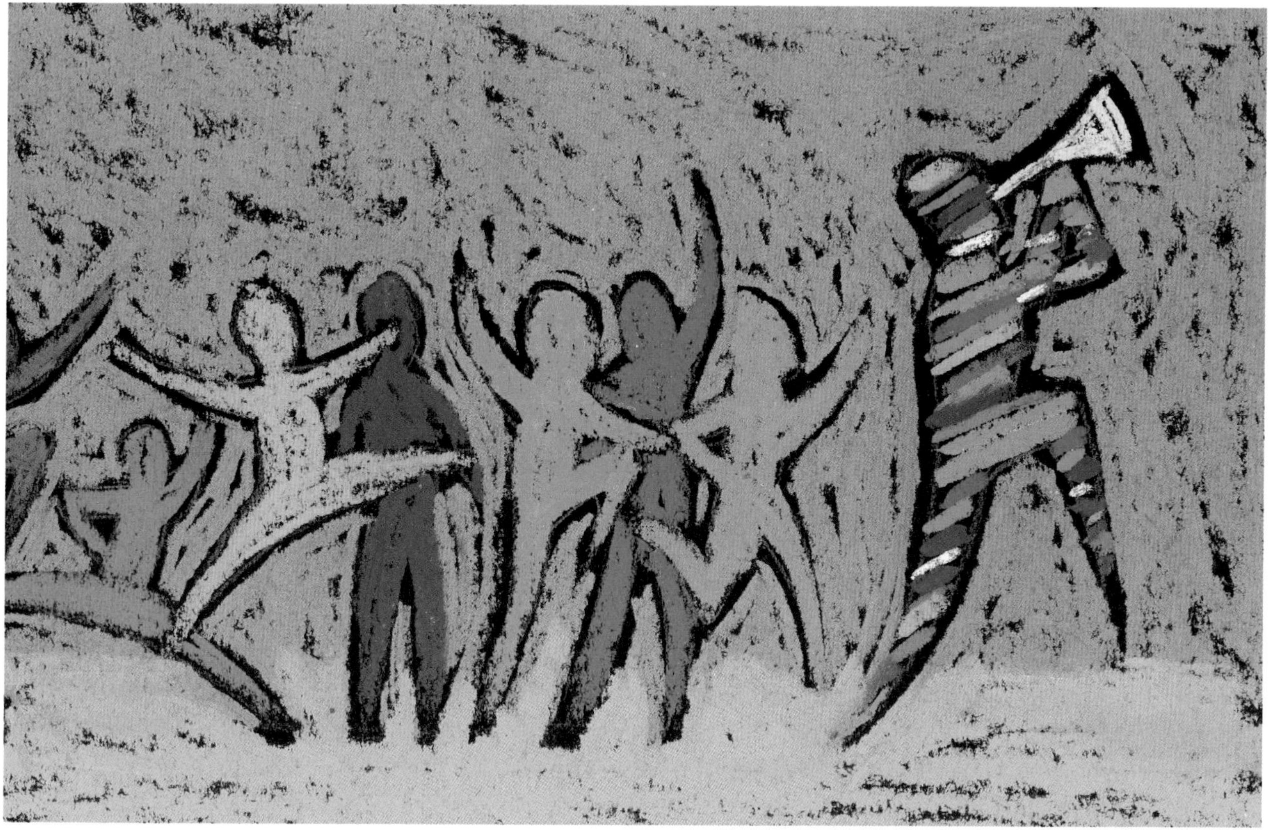

*m*y flexibility keeps me from getting bent out of shape

my laugh lines are life lines

i listen to my heart

i have an attitude of gratitude

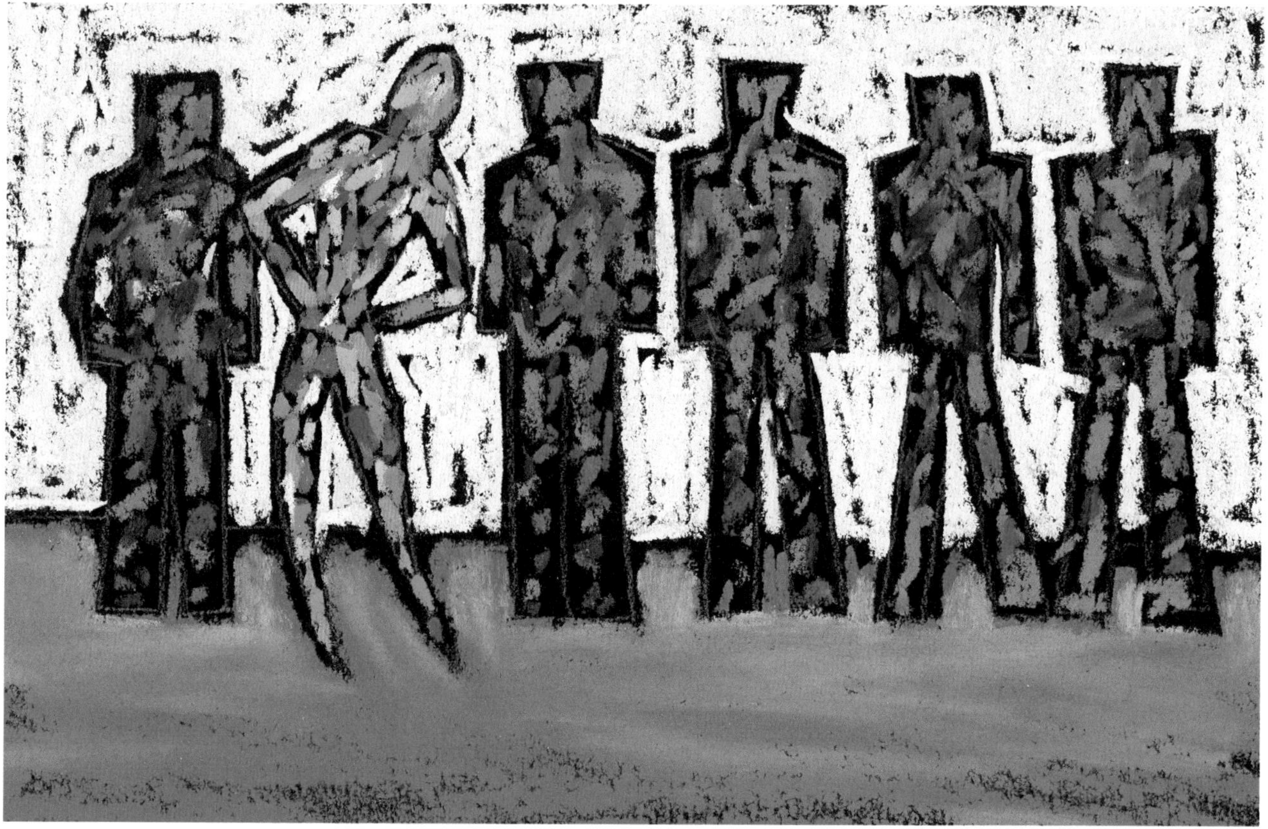

You have a bounce in your step
your chuckle chimes with the world
you live and breathe goodness
your cheerfulness is a parasol

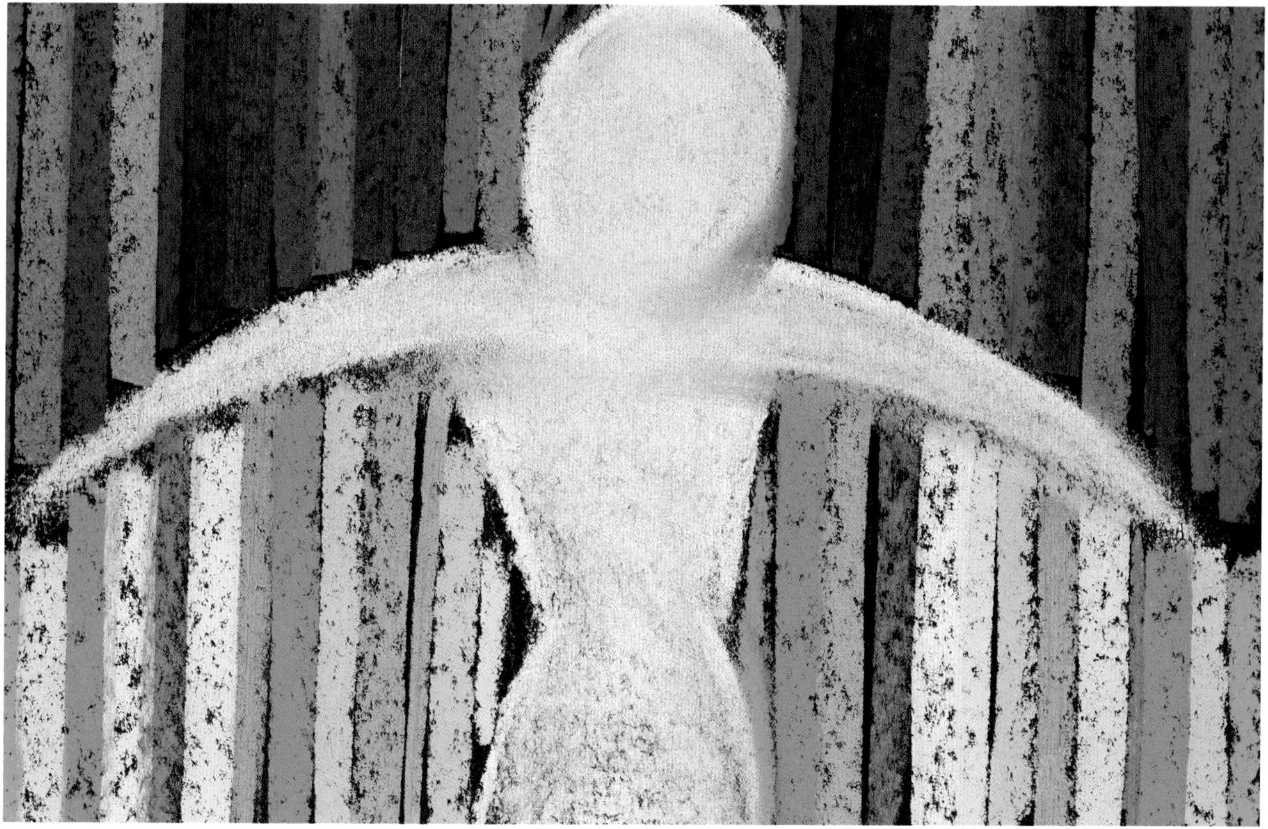

*m*y tears are raindrops for my spirit

my sadness moistens the soil for new intimacies to grow

my vulnerability is the source of my strength

my grieving fuels the forward movement of my life

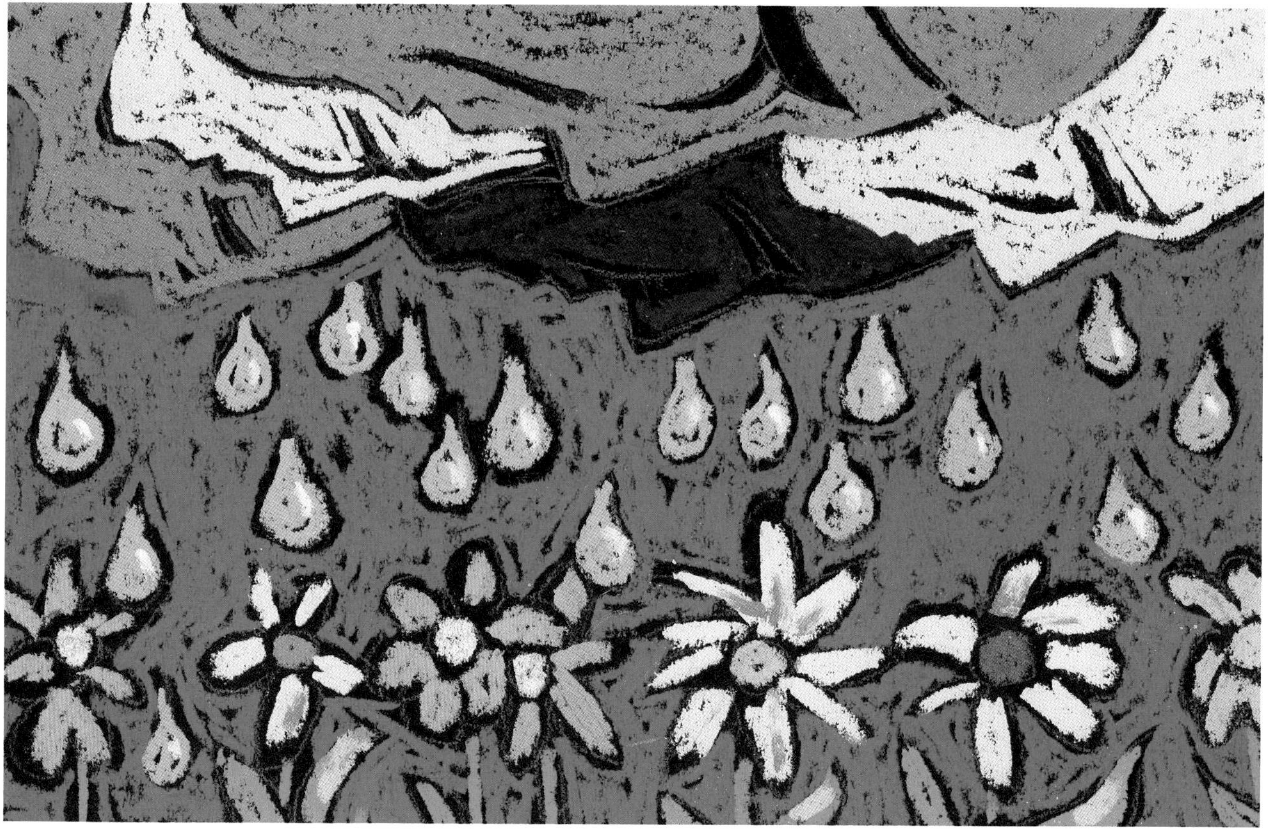

My anger is a bonfire of my strength and passion

my rage empowers my outrage against abuse

my fear is the threshold of my courage

my sense of shame is the bedrock of my honor

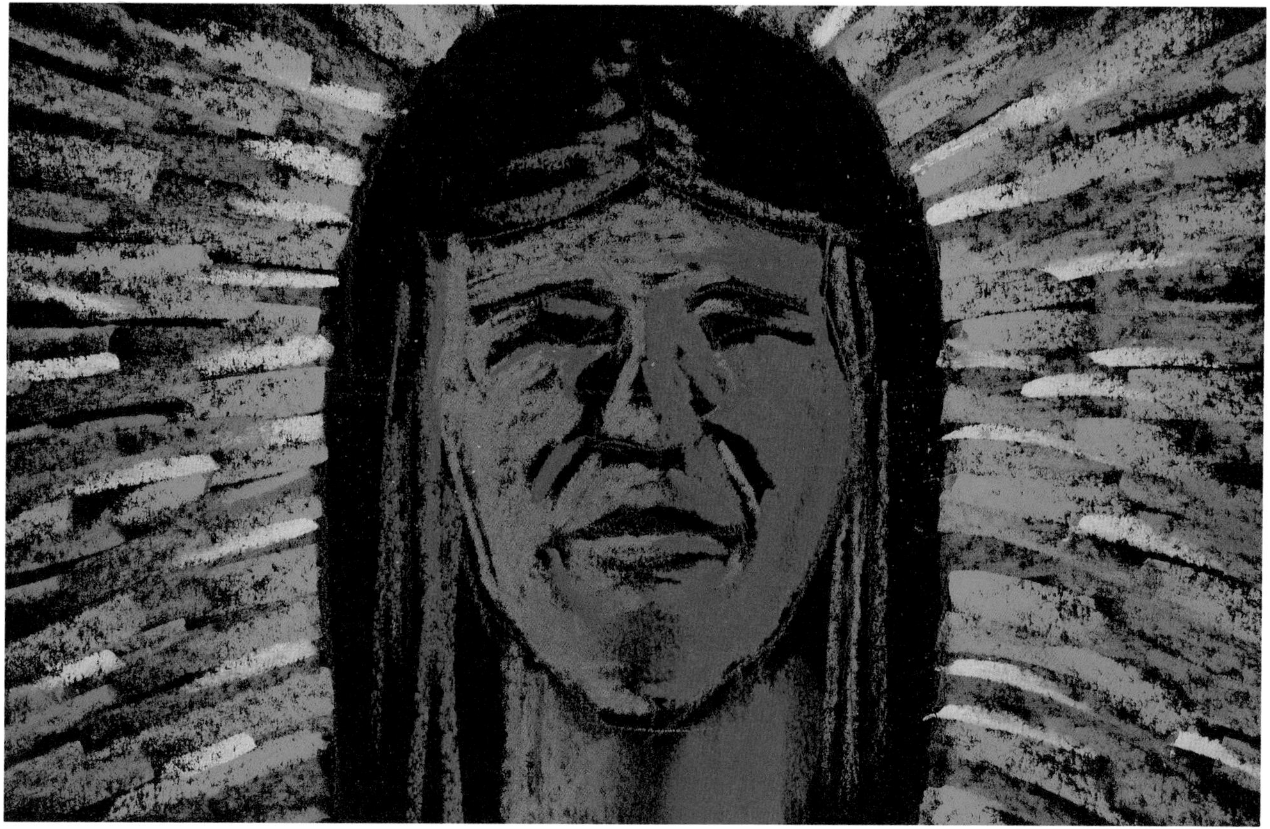

Your work has meaning

you are a person of integrity

i bask in your glow

you are a gift

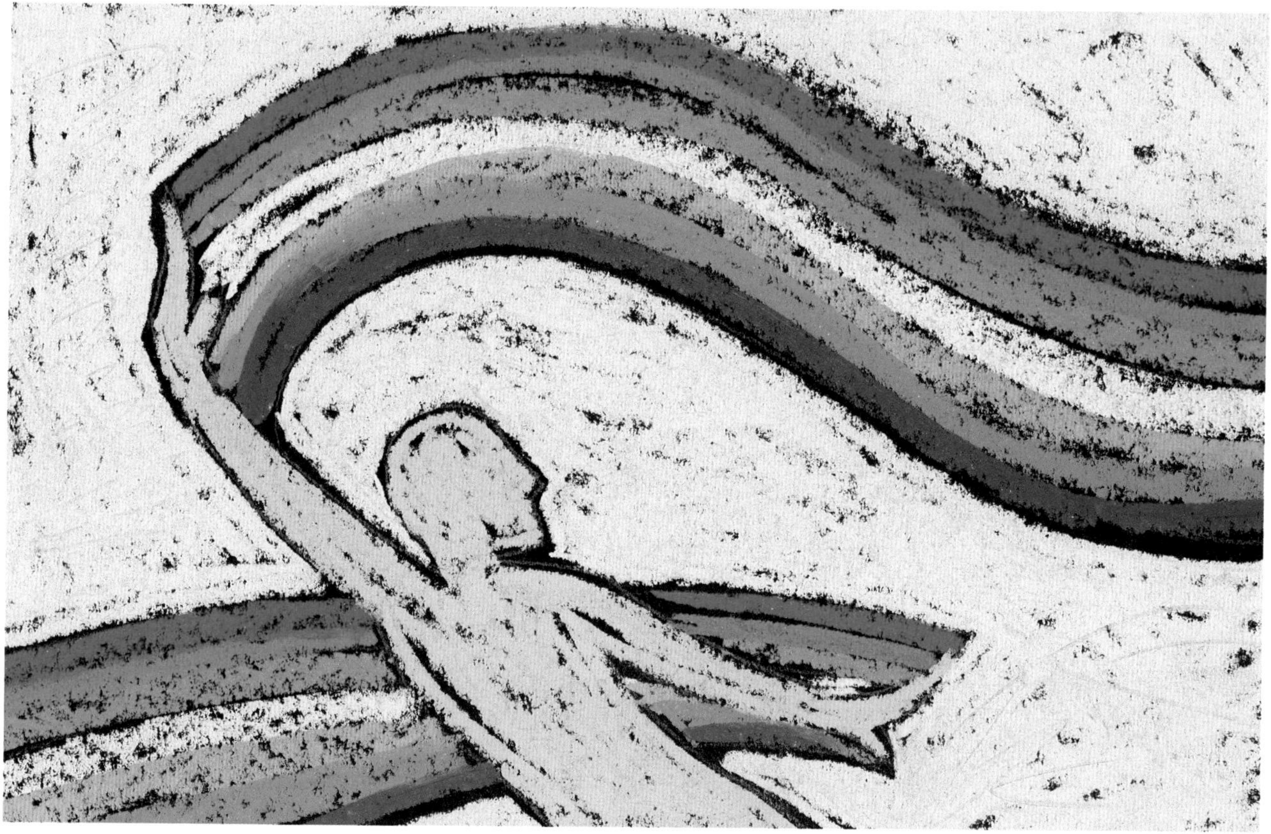

i am neat

i am discreet

i am easy to meet

i do not cheat

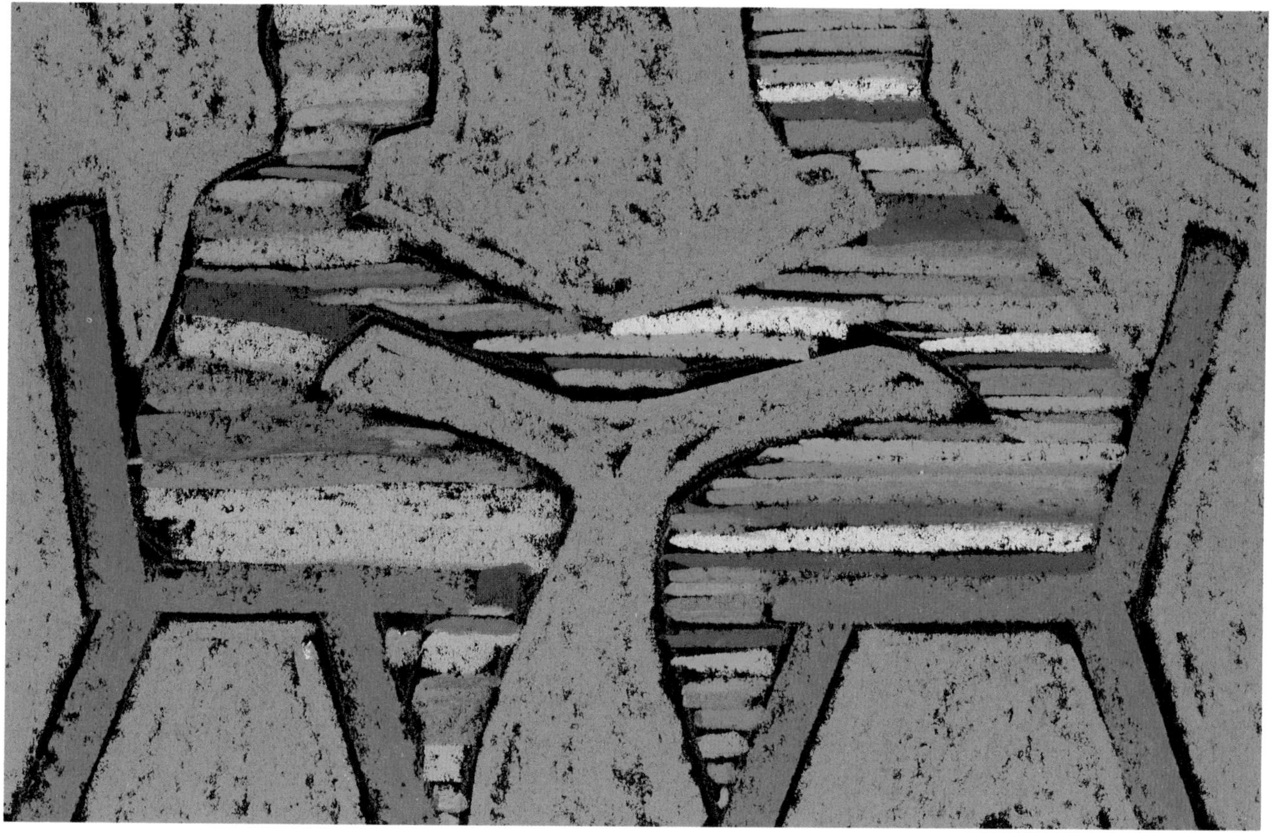

You must be proud
good job!
you have a healthy glow
you are a puddle of pleasure

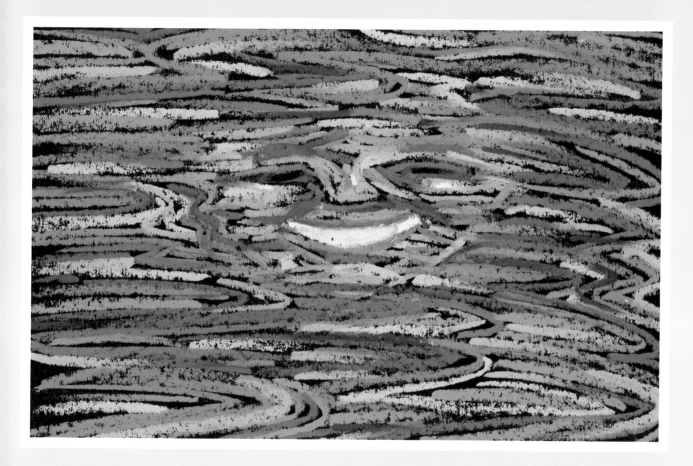

My energy astounds me

i move with grace

my heart soars

my thoughts and words are important

what i say reflects who i am

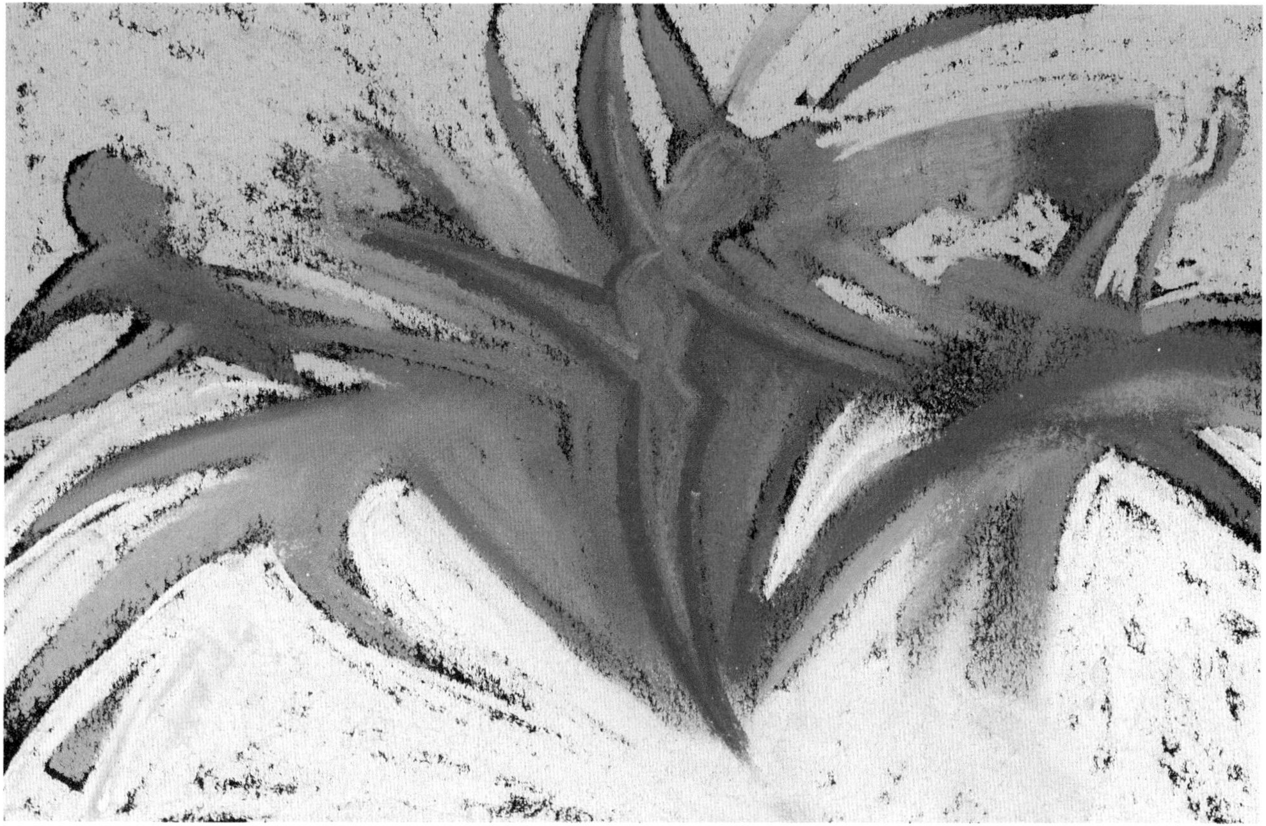

i'm a dancin' fool

i please myself

i am active and alive

i am an athlete

i am gentle with my body

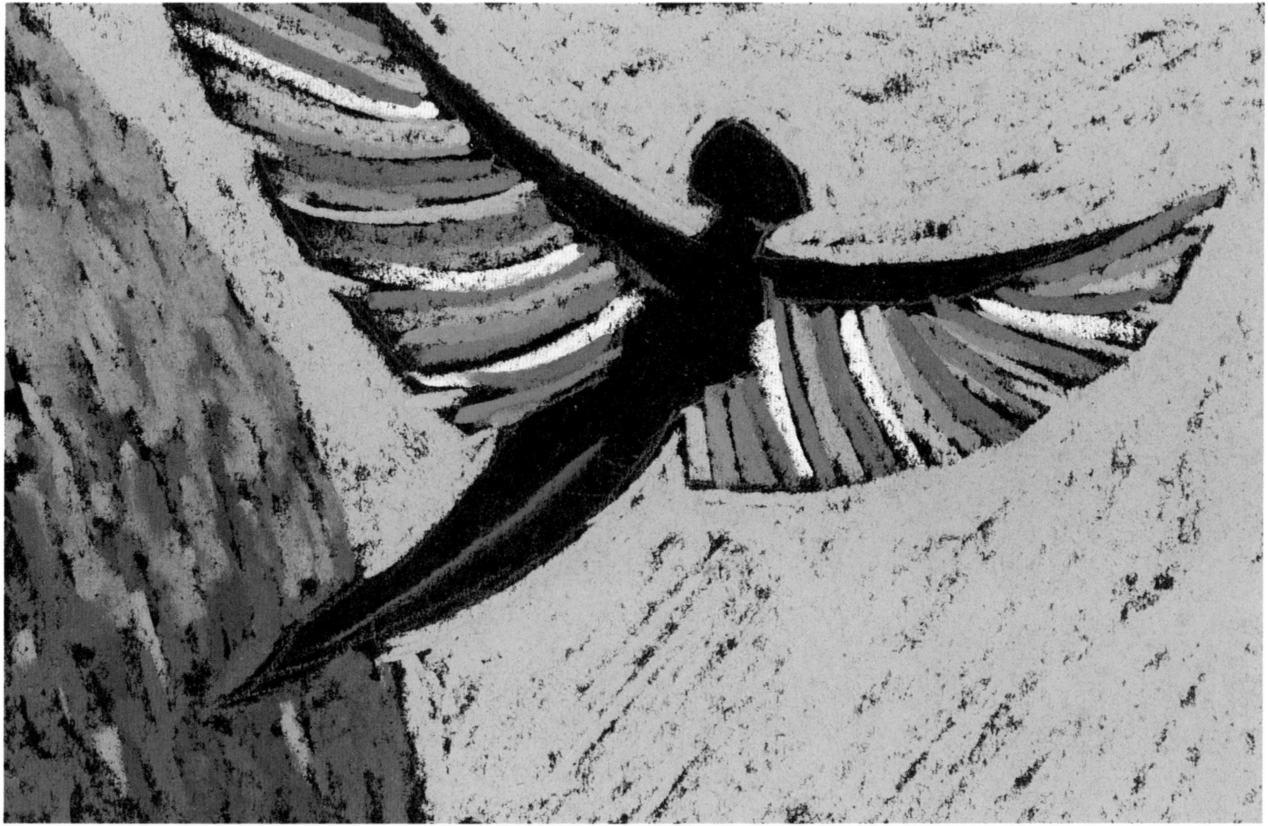

Your friends reflect your soul

your respect for our planet is refreshing

the world needs more people like you

your life is a prayer

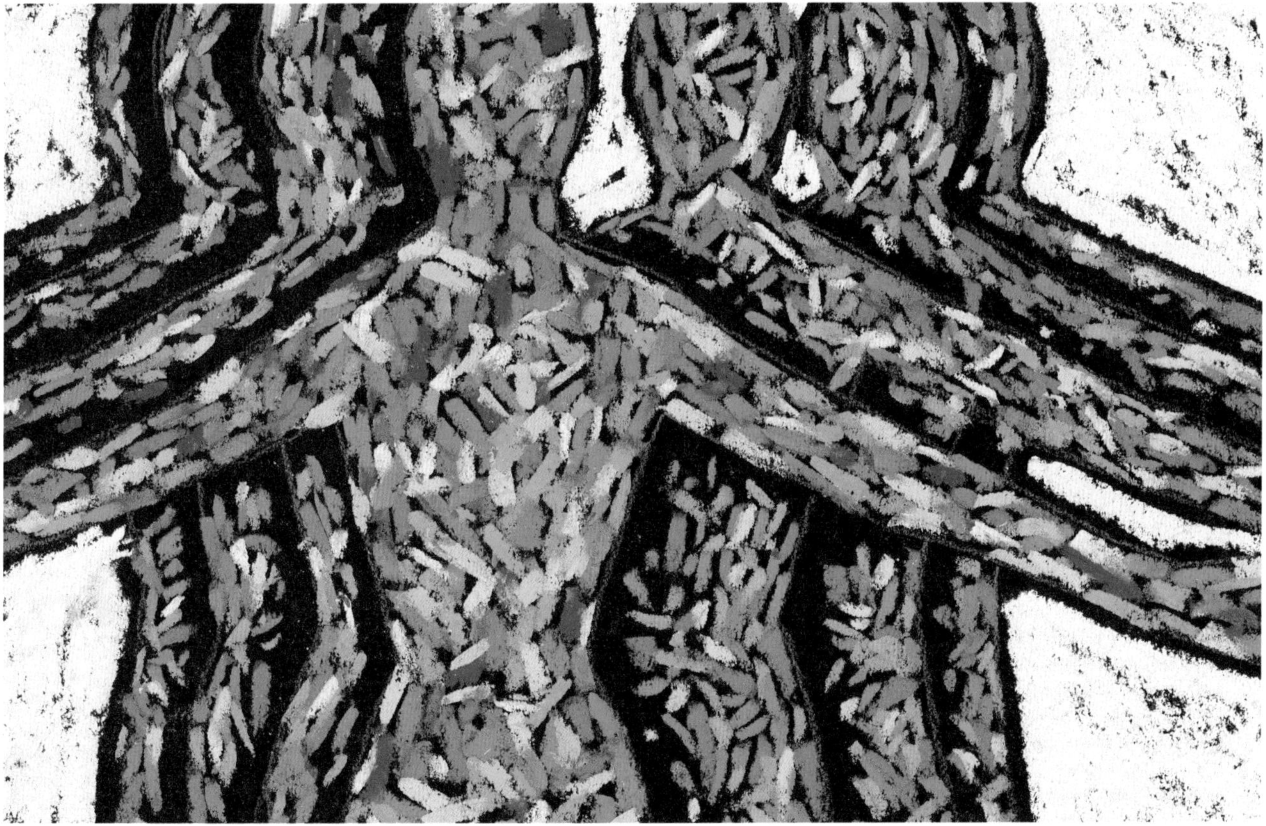

God threw away the mold after me

i accept me as i am today

the only time is right now

i am a guardian of creation

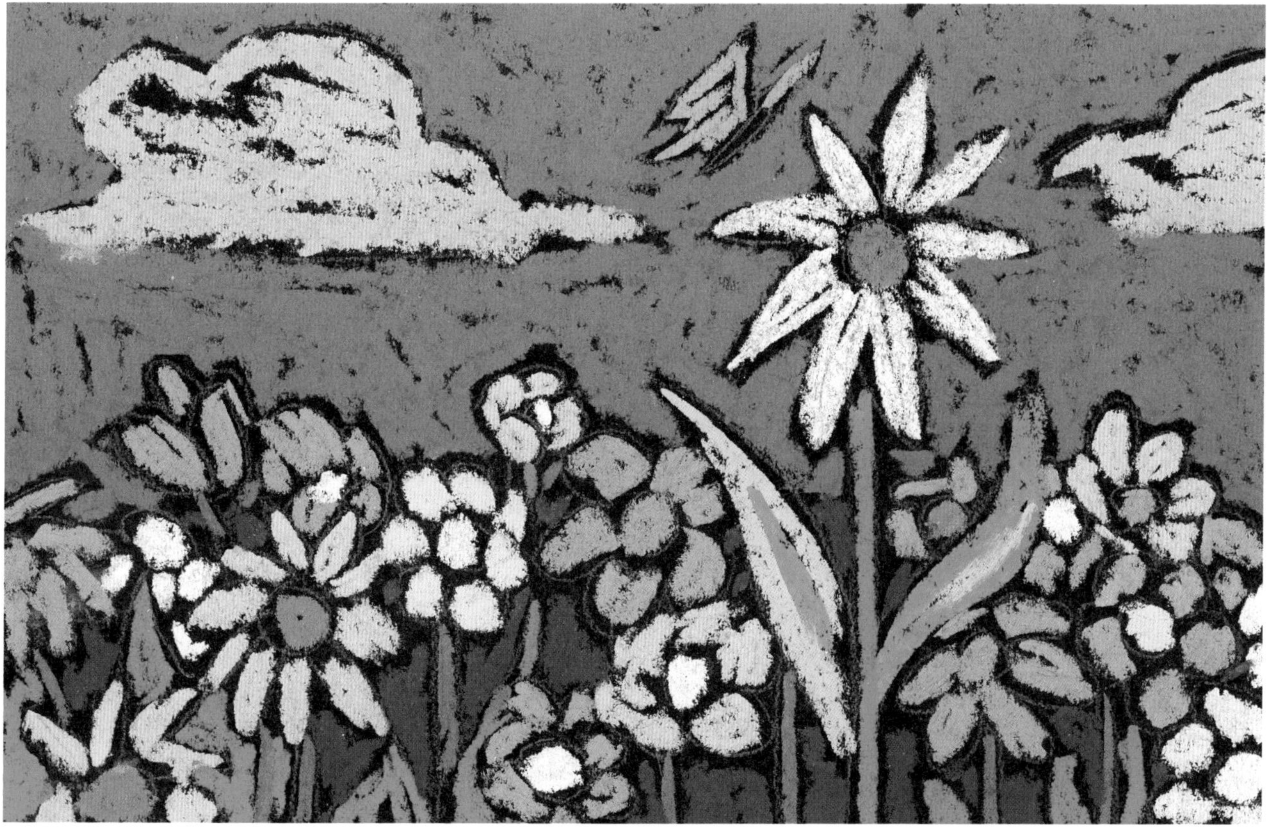

God was watching when our paths crossed
i feel safe with you
what a difference you make in my life
we bring out the best in each other

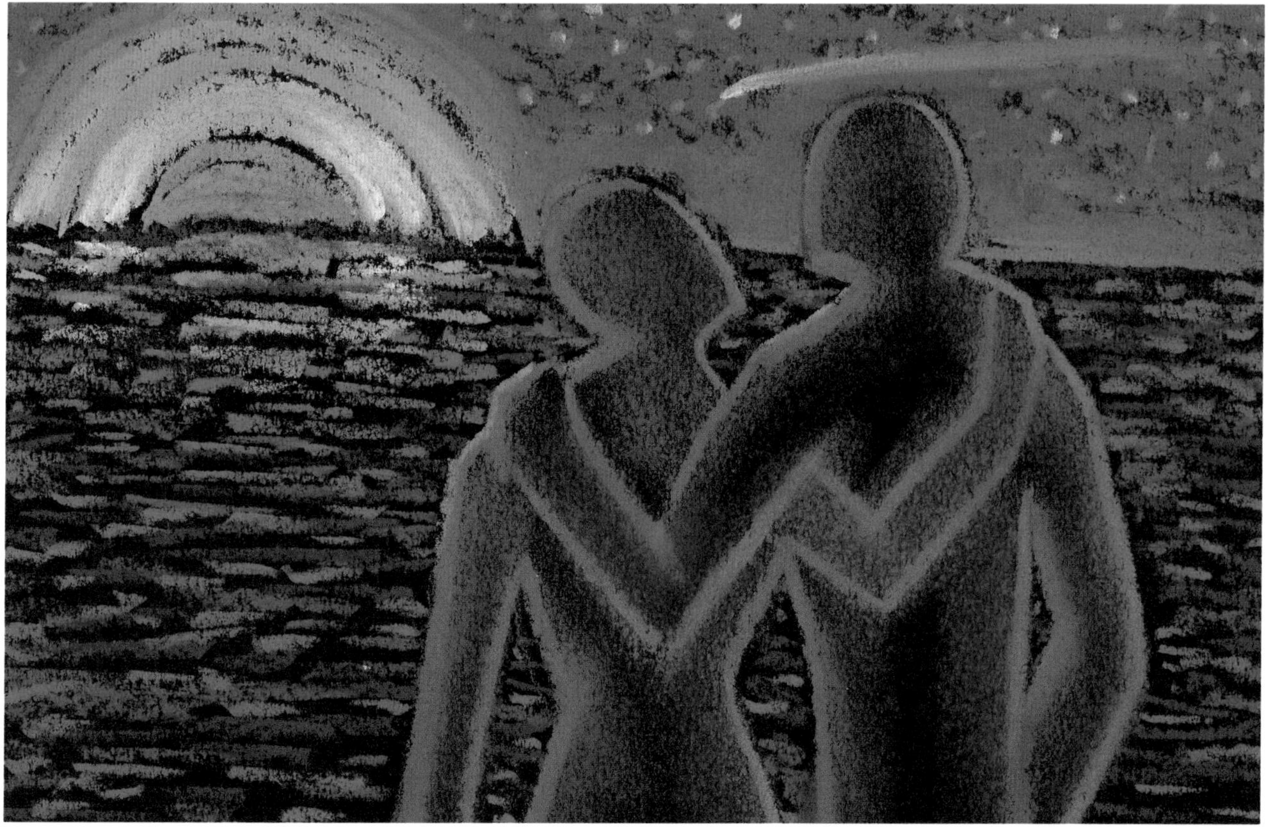

You speak with poetry

you draw with inspiration

you write with charm

you sing with beauty

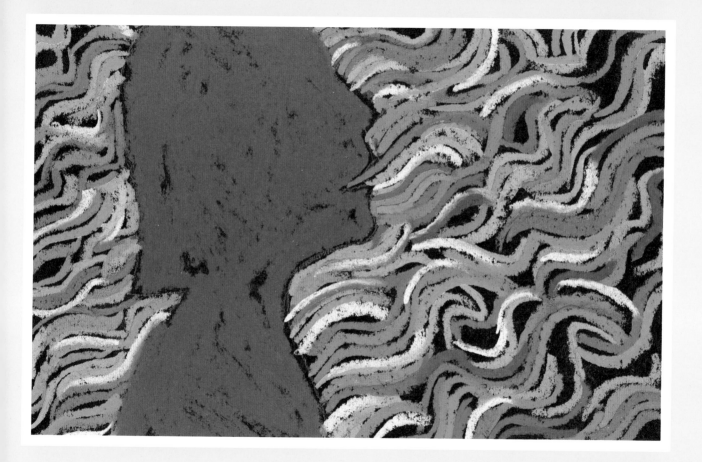

*m*y life is the journey i keep beginning

my journal is the story of my journey

my journey is my destination

i have arrived

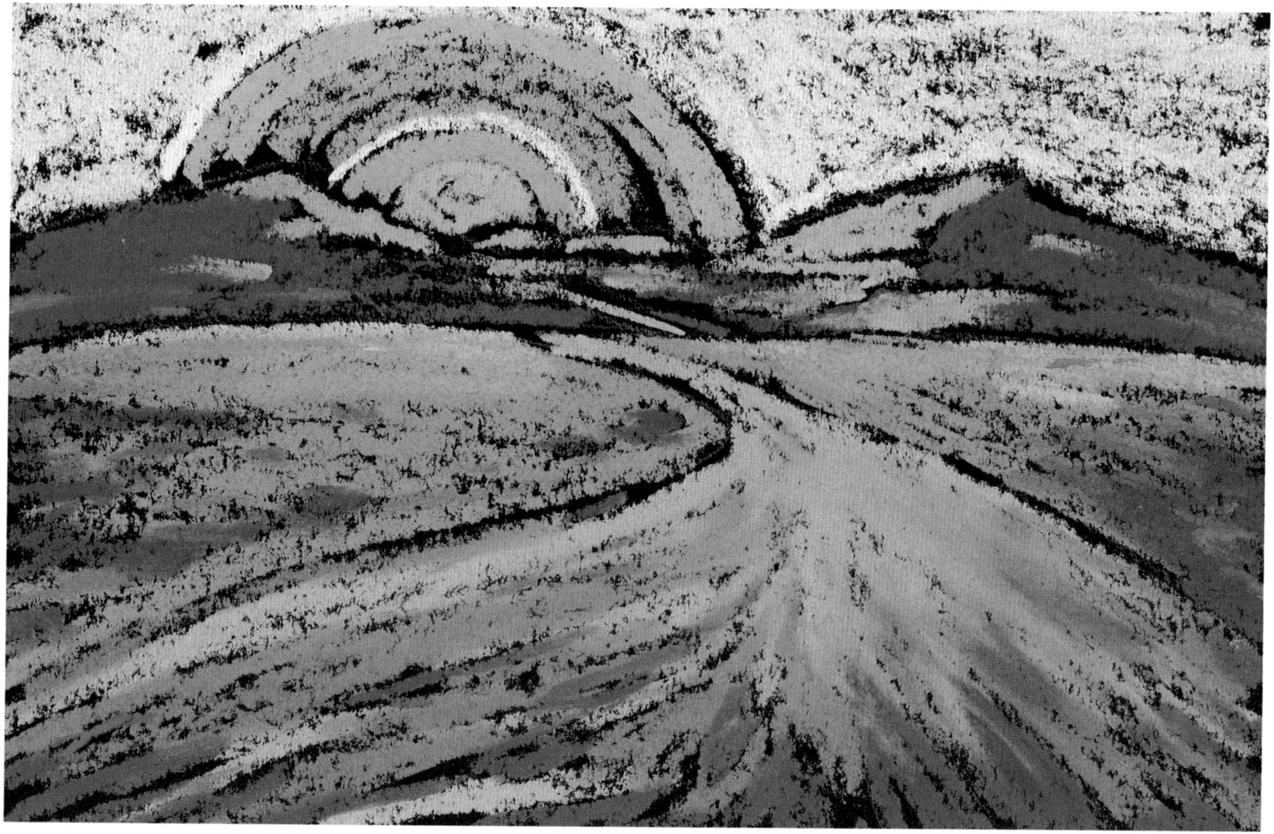

Marvel Harrison, a native of Canada, is an avid runner, skier, canoeist and likes to play. She is a PhD candidate in Counseling Psychology, author, therapist and lecturer specializing in a gentle approach to self acceptance. She is an eating disorder consultant and a program trainer for Baywood Hospital in Webster, Texas. Marvel's spirit and zest for life are easily felt by audiences everywhere.

Terry Kellogg is a parent, athlete, counselor and teacher. For twenty years he has been helping families with compulsive and addictive behaviors. Besides writing poetry, he is a wilderness enthusiast, an advocate for vulnerable groups and our planet. He is a national education consultant and a trainer for Baywood Hospital in Webster, Texas. Terry is an entertaining, challenging, inspiring and much sought after speaker.

Gregory Michaels is a full time Dad and a free lance illustrator. His clever wit and sensitivity to children of all ages are apparent in his work and he has a terrific sense of humor to boot! Greg and his family make their home in the Rocky Mountains of Colorado.